D0847437

Sports Stars

DWIGHT GOODEN

King of the Ks

By Bert Rosenthal

 CHILDRENS PRESS ®
CHICAGO

Cover photograph: Chuck Solomon
Inside photographs courtesy of the following:
Ira Golden, pages 6, 12, 21, 27, 29, 31, and 40
George Gojkovich, pages 9, 14, 16, 23, 34, 37, and 42
Bryan Yablonsky, page 19
Chuck Solomon, page 25

Library of Congress Cataloging in Publication Data

Rosenthal, Bert.
  Dwight Gooden.

  (Sport stars)
  Summary: Traces the life and baseball career of the New
York Mets pitcher, known as "Dr. K." for his many strikeouts.
  1. Gooden, Dwight—Juvenile literature.
2. Baseball players—United States—Biography—Juvenile
literature. [1. Gooden, Dwight. 2. Baseball players.]
I. Title. II. Series.
GV865.G62R66 1985   796.357′092′4 [B] [92] 85-11687
ISBN 0-516-04348-X

        4 5 6 7 8 9 10 R 94 93 92 91 90 89 88 87

Sports Stars

DWIGHT GOODEN

King of the Ks

It should not have been a surprise that Dwight Gooden became one of baseball's best pitchers at a young age.

The reason? Dwight began learning about baseball when he was very young.

Dwight learned from his father, Dan.

When Dan was young, he played semipro baseball. He was a first baseman. He was a fairly good hitter.

When Dan grew older, he hoped his sons would play baseball. His first three sons did not take to the game. Then along came Dwight. He took to baseball.

When Dwight was three years old, his father was the coach of a semipro team. The team was called the Tampa Dodgers. The team played in Tampa, Florida.

Dan Gooden and his wife, Ella Mae, lived in Tampa. That's where Dwight was born on November 16, 1964.

When Dan coached the team, Dwight would often sit in the dugout with him. He began to learn about baseball.

Dwight loved the sport. When he was 6, his father took him to see an exhibition game between two major league teams. The game was played in Lakeland, Florida. The teams were the Boston Red Sox and the Detroit Tigers.

During the game, Al Kaline of Detroit hit two home runs. Dwight quickly became an Al Kaline fan.

"Dad, I want to be like Al Kaline," Dwight told his father.

Then, Dwight would get out his baseball bat. His father would pitch the ball to him easily. And Dwight would say, "I'm Al Kaline."

One day, when he still was 6, Dwight came running home from baseball practice. He had been pitching with his father. He ran up to his mother and said, "Mama, I threw a grown man out. Really, Mama. I threw a grown man out. I ain't storyin'."

Dwight started playing Little League baseball when he was 8 years old. He played shortstop and third base. His team lost often. At the end of the season, he quit.

But he came back. He played with the same team the next year. Again, the same thing happened. The team kept losing. And Dwight quit again. He was upset. He was playing hard. The other kids were "messing up."

Dan Gooden talked to Dwight about the team. He told him that the other kids also were trying hard. It wasn't their fault that they weren't able to play better.

He also told Dwight that he would let him quit *this* time. But that if he did it again, he couldn't play baseball any more.

Dwight's baseball playing days almost ended at age 10. That year, he was playing Little League ball again. In his first five times at bat, he failed to get a hit. Three of those times he struck out.

He told the head of the league that he wanted to quit. He said he was scared. The head helped change his mind. So Dwight then became the starting third baseman for the team. The team of mostly 11 and 12 year olds went on to play in the Little League World Series. But Dwight couldn't play. He was too young. He was only 10 years old.

Dwight's fastball can reach speeds of 95 miles per hour.

Dwight had a strong throwing arm. When he was 12 he was asked to pitch a game. In his first game as a pitcher, he did not allow any runs.

One day Dwight's father asked his son to pitch to him. He wanted to see if his son could strike him out. Dwight did it easily. He needed only three pitches to strike out his father.

That convinced Dan Gooden that Dwight might someday make a good major league pitcher.

Dwight did become a very good major league pitcher. His team was the New York Mets.

Although he has pitched some very good games for the Mets, he still remembers a game when he was only 12 years old.

In that game he did not allow any runs. He struck out 16 of 18 batters. And he hit two home runs. The game was against an arch-rival Little League team. Every seat in the stadium was filled.

"I threw my hands up in the air after one of the home runs," Dwight said. "I was so charged up I didn't go to bed that night."

When Dwight was young, his two favorite pitchers were Nolan Ryan and J.R. Richard.

"My friends always compared me with them in the Little Leagues," Dwight said. "I didn't keep their clippings or anything like that. But I watched them on TV whenever they'd pitch."

Ryan and Richard both were strikeout pitchers. They threw the ball very hard. So does Dwight.

"That doesn't mean I got caught up with striking out guys," said Dwight. "Your job is getting guys out. One way is striking them out. But I'll take every first-pitch grounder to the shortstop that I can get. It's easier on your arm."

Dwight covers first base during a double play.

Still, Dwight knew as early as age 12 that he could throw hard. For a boy that age, he had big, strong legs. Legs are very important to a pitcher. Big, strong legs help a pitcher drive off the mound hard. Driving off the mound hard helps a pitcher throw harder.

When Dwight went to high school, he did not pitch on the school team during his first two years. Instead, he pitched for a good team in the Senior National League. That league was for boys 14 to 18 years old. Dwight's father had told his son not to play for the school team. The team had a lot of seniors. He did not think Dwight would play much.

In 1984, Dwight struck out 276 batters in 218 innings.

But when Dwight was a junior in Hillsborough High School, he became the team's No. 2 pitcher. In his senior year, he was No. 1.

In his high school career, Dwight won 14 games. He lost only four. He also struck out 130 batters in 74 innings. That's an average of nearly two each inning—a very high average.

In high school, Dwight also was given the name of "The Doctor." One reason he got that name was because he liked the basketball player Julius Erving. Julius Erving's nickname is "Dr. J."

The K corner in Shea Stadium. Each time Dwight strikes out a batter, the fans add a K. When Dwight is pitching, the K corner is busy.

Dr. J. operates very well on the court with a basketball. Dwight operates very well on the mound with a baseball.

Later, Dwight's nickname became "Dr. K." The K stands for strikeouts. A K is a short way of noting a strikeout when keeping score in baseball. Mets fans even have a K corner. Dwight's fans sit in this corner. Every time Dwight makes a strikeout, the fans display a K.

Dwight finished high school in the spring of 1982. In June 1982, he was chosen by the Mets in baseball's free agent draft. He was the fifth player chosen overall.

When Dwight signed with the Mets, he was given a bonus of $85,000. He also was assigned to the Mets' Kingsport, Tennessee team in the Rookie League. At Kingsport, he pitched nine games. He won five. He lost four. He also struck out 66 batters in 66 innings. Again, a very good average.

Before the 1982 season ended, the Mets sent Dwight to their Little Falls team in the New York-Penn League. He pitched in only two games for Little Falls. He lost his only decision. But again he was good with strikeouts. This time, he struck out 18 batters in 13 innings.

Even as a child, Dwight was fascinated with baseball.

In 1983 Dwight was promoted to Lynchburg of the Carolina League. At Lynchburg, Dwight was sensational. He won 19 games. He lost only four. He also hurled 6 shutouts. He had an earned run average of 2.50. He struck out 300 batters in 191 innings. That was an amazing total.

The next year, 1984, the Mets invited Dwight to their spring training camp in St. Petersburg, Florida. He was not expected to make the major league team that year. But the Mets' new manager that year was Dave Johnson.

Johnson had seen Dwight pitch in 1983. He had made a promise then. His promise was, "Wherever I'm managing in 1984, that kid will be my opening day pitcher."

Nelson Doubleday, chairman of the board of the New York Mets, congratulates Dwight for winning the Rookie of the Year Award.

Johnson also said, "This is the best pitching prospect I ever saw. And I saw Jim Palmer when he came up with the Baltimore Orioles."

Palmer was one of the best pitchers in baseball history. Before he retired in 1984, he won the Cy Young Award as the best pitcher in the American League three times.

The Mets had planned to send Gooden to the minor leagues in 1984. They thought he needed more seasoning. But at Johnson's request, they kept him. It was a very wise decision.

By the end of the season, Dwight was named the National League's Rookie of the Year. At only 19 years of age, he was the youngest ever to win the award. In the voting by the Baseball Writers' Association of America, he received 23 of a possible 24 first-place votes.

The announcement of the award was made on the birthday of Dwight's father, Dan.

"You have only one chance to win this award, and to win it is a great honor," Dwight said. "And to win it especially on my father's birthday."

Dwight deserved the award. In his first season in the major leagues, he won 17 games. He lost only nine. He also had a 2.60 earned run average. He set many records. Most of them were strikeout records.

He set a major league record for rookies with 276 strikeouts. The old record was 245. It was set by Herb Score of the Cleveland Indians in 1953.

Dwight set a major league record for strikeouts per 9 innings. Dwight's strikeout average per 9 innings was 11.39. The old record was 10.71. That was set by Sam McDowell of Cleveland in 1965.

Dwight set a Mets' rookie record with 16 strikeouts in one game. He tied a major league record with 32 strikeouts in two straight games. And he set a major league record with 43 strikeouts in three straight games.

He also set a Mets' record by striking out 10 or more batters in 15 games. And he set a Mets' record with five straight games of 10 or more strikeouts.

He also became the youngest player to be selected for baseball's All-Star Game. In that game he struck out all three batters he faced in his first inning.

During one stretch late in the season, Dwight won 7 straight starts. In one of those games, he pitched a one-hitter against the Chicago Cubs. The only hit off him was an infield single.

Dwight relaxes and stretches his 6 foot 4 inch frame.

"I still can't believe all the nice things that happened to me in 1984," Dwight said. "In the spring, I had been just a non-roster player hoping to win a spot on the team."

But he knew in his first outing that he belonged in the major leagues.

"My first game was great," he said. "Facing all those hitters I'd watched on TV, I knew right there I could make it."

His second game was not so great. It was against Chicago. And he lasted only 3 1/3 innings. After that game, Dwight was upset. He called his father.

"Dwight said, 'Maybe I lost it,' " Dan Gooden said. "If I hadn't been talking to him, he might have really started thinking it."

Dwight didn't stay upset long. Two weeks later he was pitching in a game against the Montreal Expos. The bases were loaded. And there were no outs. But Dwight pitched out of trouble by striking out Gary Carter, Andre Dawson, and Tim Raines. Those were the Expos' three best hitters.

"I got this big feeling all over," Dwight said. "I got hyper inside. I had the ball in my hand and I did it."

Dwight set a Mets' record by striking out 10 or more batters in 15 games.

Dwight did things very well the rest of the season.

"Dwight Gooden just hates to lose at anything." said his manager, Dave Johnson. "That's why he is just going to keep getting better and better as the years go on."

"I just want to win as many games as I can," Dwight said. "And help the team finish as high as it can."

The higher the team finishes and the better Dwight pitches, the more money he will make. For his first season in the major leagues, he was paid $40,000. That is the least amount of money a rookie can be paid.

Dwight and his teammate, outfielder Darryl Strawberry, sit in the bull pen.

After his remarkable rookie season, he signed a new contract. It was worth $325,000 a year. Dwight could also make $150,000 in bonus money.

In 1985 Dwight again amazed the baseball world. He led the major leagues—24 wins, 268 strikeouts, and an ERA of only 1.53. At the end of the year, Dwight received the Cy Young Award. It seemed that nothing could stop him.

Then came 1986.

Dwight started to get into trouble. He missed meetings. He missed appointments. People knew he was having problems, but Dwight always said everything was fine.

On the field, Dwight was still a great pitcher. But he wasn't as good as he had been. He was voted the best National League pitcher, though, when the All-Star team was picked.

Dwight had problems. But the Mets were winning and people didn't pay much attention.

Dwight continued to miss appointments. He even had troubles with the police. He wasn't hanging around with the right people.

Then, just as the 1987 season was ready to begin, Dwight failed a drug test. He stopped playing baseball and checked himself into an alcoholism and drug treatment center. It was a good decision. There, he could get help.

Dwight Gooden had become a national hero and celebrity. He was very young. But all that fame and money were not making him happy.

People talked with Dwight. He said he just wanted to solve his problems and go back to playing baseball. His teammates and fans were on his side. "We do *love* him," said fellow pitcher Bob Ojeda.

CHRONOLOGY

1964   —Dwight Gooden is born on November 16 in Tampa, Florida.

1967   —His father, Dan, becomes coach of a semipro baseball team, and takes Dwight to the games with him.

1970   —Dan takes Dwight to an exhibition game, and they see Al Kaline of Detroit hit two home runs.

1972   —At age 8, Dwight begins playing Little League baseball.

1976   —Dwight switches from being a third baseman to a pitcher, and doesn't allow any runs in his first game.

1976   —Dwight pitches a shutout, strikes out 16 of 18 batters, and hits two home runs in a memorable game against an arch-rival Little League team.

1981-82 —In his junior and senior seasons in Hillsborough High School, Dwight compiles a 14-4 record with 130 strikeouts in 74 innings.

1982   —The New York Mets choose Dwight in baseball's free agent draft.

1983   —In his first full season in professional baseball, Dwight posts a 19-4 record with 300 strikeouts for a Mets' minor league team.

1984   —Dwight makes it with the Mets. And he makes it big. In his first season with the major league team, he finishes with a 17-9 record and a 2.60 earned run average. He also sets a major league record for rookies with 276 strikeouts. He sets a major league record for strikeout per nine innings with an average of 11.39. He ties a major league record with 32 strikeouts in two straight games. He sets a major league record with 43 strikeouts in three straight games. At age 19, he is the youngest player selected for baseball's All-Star Game. And he is named the National League's Rookie of the Year, receiving 23 of a possible 24 first-place votes.

1985   —Dwight becomes the youngest pitcher to ever receive the Cy Young Award. He finishes the season with a record of 24-4 and leads the National League in earned run average, strikeouts (268), complete games, and innings pitched.

1986   —For the third straight year, Dwight is selected to the All-Star Game team. This time he is the National League starting pitcher.

       —Dwight's Mets reach the World Series, and win. But Dwight loses his two starts, Game Two 9 to 3 and Game Five 4 to 2. Dwight is unhappy and misses the parade after his team wins the World Series over Boston.

1987   —Dwight enters an alcohol and drug treatment center just as the season is ready to begin.

ABOUT THE AUTHOR

Bert Rosenthal has worked for The Associated Press for more than 25 years. He has covered or written about virtually every sport. Mr. Rosenthal is the author of Sports Stars books on Larry Bird, Marques Johnson, Sugar Ray Leonard, Darryl Dawkins, Wayne Gretzky, Isiah Thomas, Carl Lewis, and Ralph Sampson. He is also the author of New True Books on Soccer and Basketball.

He was AP's pro basketball editor from 1973 until 1976. From 1974 until 1980, he was the secretary-treasurer of the Professional Basketball Writers' Association of America. He has been a co-author on two books—*Pro Basketball Superstars of 1974* and *Pro Basketball Superstars of 1975*. For seven years, Mr. Rosenthal was the editor of *Hoop* Magazine, an official publication of the National Basketball Association.

At present, he is the AP's track and field editor, and a frequent contributor to many basketball, football, and baseball magazines. He also has covered three Olympic Games—the 1976 Olympics at Montreal, the 1980 Games at Moscow, and the 1984 Olympics at Los Angeles.